FLEETWOOD CENTRAL

AUTHOR

ROTHWELL, C.

CLASS

E02

TITLE Fleetwood in old photographs

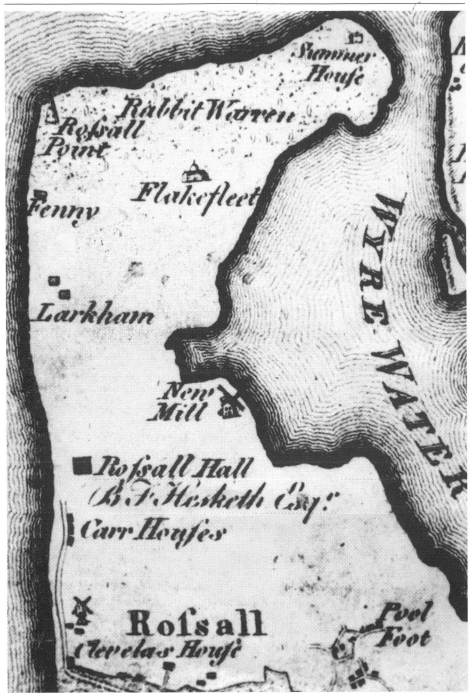

Yates's 1786 map showing Rossall Warren, the site of Fleetwood-on-Wyre.

Fleetwood

IN OLD PHOTOGRAPHS

CATHERINE ROTHWELL

Alan Sutton Publishing Limited
Phoenix Mill · Far Thrupp · Stroud
Gloucestershire

First Published 1994

Copyright © Catherine Rothwell 1994

British Library Cataloguing in Publication Data.
A catalogue record for this book is available from
the British Library.

ISBN 0-7509-0732-0

Typeset in 9/10 Sabon.
Typesetting and origination by
Alan Sutton Publishing Limited.
Printed in Great Britain by
The Guernsey Press Company Limited,
Guernsey, Channel Islands.

06376330

Contents

ONWARD

FLEETWOOD.

The first coat of arms for the town of Fleetwood.

Introduction

Both Yates's map of 1786 and Greenwood's of 1818 mark 'Rabbit Warren' as being the site upon which the unique town of Fleetwood was built. ('Fleetwood' at that time was the name of a farm.) In 1824 'Rabbit Warren' was valued at £50 and yet it was not long before 'a beautiful town was from the wilderness won'.

In the 1830s Peter Hesketh's Rossall estate was a desolate tract, home to thousands of rabbits and sea birds. The line of marram grass-covered dunes disappeared as the sea continually encroached, until only the largest remained. Lord of the Manor and High Sheriff of the County of Lancaster, Peter Hesketh, having at the age of 24 inherited nearly a third of the coastline between Formby Point and north of the Wyre in addition to rolling acres inland, had good reason to believe that the site held the makings of a sea port and a pleasant resort. Both were badly needed in the north-west. The river was a haven for ships ('safe and easy as Wyre Water' was a centuries-old proverb), and on a clear day views across Morecambe Bay to the Lake District mountains were breath-taking. If only the railway could be brought from busy Preston, booming with all the Industrial Revolution had to offer! How the workers would revel in escaping the grime and the din!

The Preston and Wyre Prospectus and Plans, published in 1834, showed a formidable list of directors. All Fylde men of substance, they were: Fitzherbert Brockholes of Claughton Hall; Daniel Elletson of Parrox Hall; Richard Harrison, owner of Little Singleton; Wilson Ffrance of Rawcliffe Hall; John Bourne, owner of Stalmine; the Horrocks brothers, cotton spinners of Preston; and Thomas Birley, flax merchant of Kirkham. However, the burghers of Preston, fearing a threat to the trade of their own town, were acrimonious towards Peter Hesketh who was also their MP.

On 15 July 1840 a single track line became reality, following the formation of the Preston and Wyre Railway, Harbour and Dock Company. Houses, churches, hotels, shops and a wharf sprang up. Fishermen were coaxed from Southport, artisans flocked from all over the Fylde and businessmen came from London like bees swarming round a honey pot.

Designed by the famous architect Decimus Burton, it was essentially a planned town with spacious thoroughfares marked out by plough. Specialists at the height of their professions were employed. From London Euston the traveller was conveyed to the North Euston Hotel at Fleetwood and thence to Belfast, Londonderry, Ardrossan, Barrow and the Isle of Man. A rail route over Shap Fell was then undreamed of but engineer Joseph Locke was to achieve it only a few years later.

As for visitors, lists of the nobility appeared in the *Fleetwood Chronicle*. Some took up residence in Upper Queen's Terrace, staying from three weeks to three months. Breakfast at the North Euston Hotel was 2s. and a bedroom was 4s. a day. During Whit Week in 1844 thousands of day trippers travelled on half fares offered by the railway company. For some it meant the first sight of the sea in their lives, and numbers topped 60,000. The largest Sunday School trip was in 1846 when two engines and fifty-six carriages brought 4,200 children and adults. There were pony and donkey rides, sea trips in yachts and steamers, the ninety-four steps of Pharos lighthouse to be climbed, dancing in the Mount hollow, regattas, sea-bathing (though all and sundry complained of the hiring charge for the bathing vans), wrestling, gingling and cricket matches. Large marquees were pitched on the Warren from where coffee and buns were given out. But the boom years were short-lived. By 1847 a branch line had been built to Blackpool, where the attractions of pleasure domes and intensive catering succeeded in enticing large numbers away.

George Landmann's estimate for the cost of the Preston and Wyre Railway had been horribly wrong. Storms, poor workmanship and misapplication of funds had all wreaked havoc and even Sir Peter (he was knighted in 1838) and his great wealth was not equal to the strain. Rossall Hall was leased, the contents being sold in a fortnight-long sale. Special trains were run on the very railway that brought him close to ruin. After Sir Peter's departure control of the township was vested in a group of commissioners. Years of struggle lay ahead.

Recession in the early years was blamed largely on the lack of a true dock, but not until 2 June 1869 did the last surviving trustee under the will of Sir Peter Hesketh Fleetwood, Harry Styan, cut the first sod. Insufficient money meant further delay and when work went ahead in 1871 history was to repeat itself: John Hawksworth, the chief engineer, gave an estimate which was wide of the mark. When work was completed the residents indulged their pride in a grand procession. Among those taking part were the First Dragoon Guards, the Local Board, various members of the gentry, the Fire Brigade, Lifeboat men, ships' carpenters, sailmakers, bricklayers, fishermen (complete with boat), Thomas Riley's sawmill staff, stonemasons and many others – the procession was a mile long. A special bronze medal, depicting a three-masted barque and a railway engine was struck. Visitors poured into the town. The £52,000 grain elevator arose (£60 was spent inlaying the date 1882, visible over a mile away). Shipments of timber, iron ore, grain, flax, livestock and general cargo arrived. The first ship in Wyre Dock was the *Armstrong* and in 1889 when *Stormcock* brought a load of mackerel and kippers Fleetwood's great fishing industry came into the ascendancy.

The sea defences, completed in 1962 and since vastly improved by EEC aid, were likewise won only after a long struggle and flooding of the town.

Billy Bridges started fishing at the age of 15 from a coal burner. He slept for'ard and washed in a bucket. He became one of the youngest top skippers during the Cod War, commanding the *Boston Blenheim*. Struggle in the face of adversity seems to epitomize the story of Fleetwood. People who love the town for its indefinable raw quality, its community spirit born of striving, return again and again. That sense of suspended animation in the air could originate from the pioneering spirit of Sir Peter, or from the anxious thoughts that went out year after year to trawlermen living dangerously on winter seas.

The Pioneers

The new promenade, opened on Saturday 10 September 1887.

W.G. Herdman's lithograph of 1839, showing the proposed site of Fleetwood Docks. In the background across the River Wyre the first two houses of the town have appeared, built by Thomas Parker, stone mason and Robert Banton, farmer. On top of the Mount, known as Tup Hill, the largest starr hill of a chain of sand dunes, the Summer House, designed by architect Decimus Burton, can be seen. The foundation stone laying ceremony for this, the commercial end of the town, was held on 7 April 1836 in front of a small crowd who raised three hearty cheers for Peter Hesketh. It followed an important meeting at Rossall Hall at which the railway, the laying out of the town and the docks were all discussed. In attendance were the Lord of the Manor, Peter Hesketh, the architect Decimus Burton and Messrs Landmann, Kemp, Lewis, Alger and Cubitt. The docks scheme, in fact, made little progress until forty years later.

St Peter's Church, Fleetwood, 1866. Rock and Company of London were at that time engaged to produce a series of engravings to promote the town. The parish church is there to this day but without its spire which had to be removed in the early 1900s because it became unsafe. The cast-iron railings were also removed. These were taken for the war effort in the early 1940s. The second building from the left, still in existence, was used as Sir Peter Hesketh's hunting lodge until sold to the customs officer Stephen Burridge Jun. By 1838 Peter Hesketh had been knighted and granted, by royal licence, the right to assume the name of Fleetwood. St Peter's Church was consecrated on 11 June 1841. As with the building of all Fleetwood's churches, whatever their denomination, the land was given by the Lord of the Manor. Sir Peter's Aunt Anna Maria of Tulketh Hall donated £500, stipulating that there had to be a tower and spire. The banker John Abel Smith gave £50 and Sir Peter gave £500. A third of the sittings were declared free and the patronage was 'to belong to Sir Peter Hesketh Fleetwood and his heirs for ever'.

Building the railway line into Fleetwood, 1839. This is one of a series of lithographs by the Liverpool artist W.G. Herdman. This trestle embankment carried the track across Kirkscar Bay to the first railway station, situated in front of the Crown Hotel. In later years when the embankment became unsafe the railway had to be re-routed around the bay.

An artist's impression of Fleetwood in 1840, based on a drawing by the architect Decimus Burton. Only part of the plan materialized. The tall Pharos lighthouse was sited elsewhere and fewer buildings were erected in the early years. There never was a statue to the founder.

Decimus Burton, the last great architect of the British classical school, *c.* 1850. So named because he was the tenth son, he lived until 1881, a bachelor devoted to his profession. He worked with his father on the building of St Leonard's-on-Sea, whose seaside terraces so pleased Peter Hesketh that he desired Decimus to design his proposed town of Fleetwood. The two men remained life-long friends, both being members of the Athenaeum Club in London and competing in archery contests at St Leonard's. Burton was one of the four shareholders in the Fleetwood Gas Company. He bought a house on Dock Street where he resided until 1844, while overseeing the planning and building work of the first years of the new town. Later he acquired land on Queen's Terrace.

The marble bust of Sir Peter Hesketh Fleetwood, Baronet, 1801–66, sculpted in Rome by H.B. Burlow in 1837. After the death of his first wife Eliza Debonnaire and all the children of that marriage Sir Peter travelled abroad. Letters to his brother the Revd Charles Hesketh vividly describe some of the experiences of his grand tour. Belgium, France, Naples, Switzerland and Spain, where he met his second wife Virginie, the daughter of Senor Pedro Garcia, are all touched upon. He wintered in Naples which he later revisited, driven to the Continent by mounting debts. 'It is cheaper living abroad. We like our new quarters where we pay half to what is done in the English quarter. We gave up all English things and have nothing but Neapolitan prices. Dear Louis goes to the Opera for one shilling – reserved seat and excellent music which is his hobby.'

Frederick Kemp, Sir Peter Hesketh Fleetwood's agent. Photographed in the 1890s, Kemp was an Essex farmer who played a big part in the early years of the town and continued to prosper long after Sir Peter's death. He was instructed to purchase any land required on the railway route from Preston to Fleetwood which did not belong to Sir Peter or to other landowners involved in the venture. Kemp became a director of the Fylde Timber Company established in 1836 and was head of the North Lancashire Steam Navigation Company. He resided at Bispham Lodge for a short time but later raised a family in the house on the corner of Victoria Street and Queen's Terrace. He was also involved as a director in the early days of the Fylde Water Works.

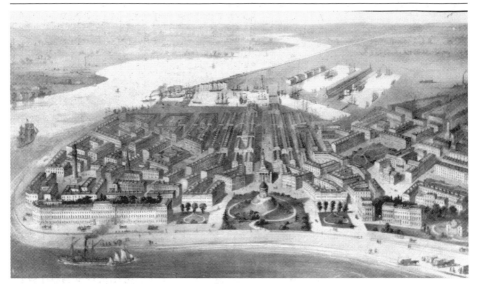

P. Gauci's bird's-eye view of Fleetwood issued with the prospectus on 25 March 1837. The prospectus stated: 'It has been determined by Mr Hesketh Fleetwood to have that portion of his estate at Rossall, in Morecambe Bay, laid out in the style of Brighton and St Leonard's.'

Sailing trawler *Milo* passing Wyre Light, *c.* 1900. Fishermen from Southport, where fishing was becoming more difficult, were persuaded to settle in Fleetwood. They brought their seamanship skills, forming a fleet of fishing smacks to help the town's commerce. Cottages were built for them in Warren Street and Upper Dock Street.

The Revd George Yarnold Osborne, vicar of Fleetwood, 1850–69, was the brother of the Revd W.A. Osborne, headmaster of Rossall School, a factor which no doubt influenced his acceptance of the living of St Peter's Parish Church. He was also personally known to his patron Sir Peter Hesketh Fleetwood. The Revd G.Y. Osborne married the sister of Mrs A. Turner, wife of the vicar of Stalmine. Never a man of strong constitution, his health was further undermined by his pioneering work in Fleetwood. In 1869 he moved to Dudley but died only two years later on 11 November 1871.

William Whiteside, or 'Billy' as he was better known, was a Fleetwood character and pioneer. As the town's bellman he settled in Fleetwood with his wife Ellen, from Skippool, in the 1840s. Billy was also bailiff, chimney sweep, glazier, billposter and sole agent for the *Fleetwood Chronicle*, which he cried in every street. The thrifty commissioners instructed Billy not to light the gas lamps on moonlit nights. His son Jack, who succeeded him as bellman, died aged 81. Jack was town crier for fifty years and saw the population rise from 3,000 to 22,000. The office of bellman became redundant on 31 October 1924.

East Street, Fleetwood, in the 1890s. On the right is St Peter's Church which required extension within a few years as the population grew. The centrally placed town lamp is where people gathered in Albert Square. Beside it is the sea-water hydrant, used for watering the streets to keep them clean. The No. 14 tram is one of the earliest types. The Blackpool and Fleetwood Tramroad Act of 1898 led to the first electric car running in July of that year. Houses on the left later had shop fronts fitted. In the distance on the right can be seen the tower of the Congregational Church which later became the site of Marks and Spencer.

Albert Square has witnessed many scenes in the history of the town: Whitsuntide, Carnival and Hospital Saturday processions, led by bands and featuring tableaux, morris dancers, decorated bicycles, well-groomed, beribboned horses, with their brasses shining like gold, have all passed through. In the nineteenth century the Christmas display in the shops of Fleetwood spared no expense. The grocers, butchers and especially H. Leadbetter in North Albert Street off the square were renowned. Judge Parry who lived in Poulton used to buy his fresh fish and lobsters at Leadbetter's shop. There is now a clock tower in place of the hydrant, in memory of Mrs Margaret Rowntree who was twice Mayor of Fleetwood.

Queen Victoria's visit to Fleetwood in September 1847. The queen and Prince Albert with the royal children called on their way back from Balmoral, Scotland, having visited the Isle of Man on the previous day. The weather was very rough and the queen, who was expecting another child, felt unwell. She set foot on Fleetwood soil, 'the newest town in all her dominions', only to walk to the royal train drawn up in front of Queen's Terrace, but the prince consort was up at 6 o'clock to climb the Mount from where he viewed the layout of the new town. The long shed on the right had been hastily erected and fitted out with velvet hangings, a dais and a gilded throne for Victoria to receive Sir Peter Hesketh Fleetwood with the High Sheriff of Lancashire and other dignitaries. The white kid gloves she was wearing and the quill pen with which she signed her name were presented to Sir Peter as mementoes of the great occasion. To this day they are preserved in the family. In later years Queen Victoria sent Sir Peter a bunch of violets after he wrote a poem for her and she also gave him a photograph of herself and family with the bust of Prince Albert in the background. Although 'the widow of Windsor' frequently gave photographs, she normally never presented any on which her deeply mourned husband appeared.

The Landmark, Rossall Point, seen here c. 1919, was pulled down in 1929. Built on the orders of the Lancaster Port Commissioners to guide their ships, it was commenced in 1767 but not completed until 1769. The cage at the top held the warning beacon. To preserve the woodwork the timbers were tarred regularly but encroaching seas washed the structure down more than once. Generations of Fleetwood boys climbed it to cut their initials into the wood. On one occasion in the fog two soldiers caught by the tide had to cling to the framework until rescued. When the town of Fleetwood was built with its two lighthouses the timber landmark was no longer required and was carted off for firewood, but the circular base can still be found covered with barnacles at Rossall Point.

Wyre Light at low tide, c. 1920. The screw pile lighthouse, part of Captain Henry Mangles Denham's charting of the approach to the port, was put up in 1840. In the early years visitors went out to it in boats to see the view, the ladies being hauled up in baskets while the men climbed the metal ladder. Designed by the blind engineer Mr Mitchell, it was shipped from Belfast on the steamer Collinge on 26 November 1830 and rapidly erected between tides by men working throughout the day and by moonlight. The first of its kind, it excited the interest of London architects and a description with engraving was printed in the Railway Magazine. Mitchell checked the construction by feeling it and discovered a flaw unnoticed by the sighted.

Rossall School, Fleetwood, in a Rock and Company engraving of 1868. Opened in 1844, the school was designed to receive the sons of clergy and of gentlemen. Nothing remains of the original Rossall Hall but a stone gazebo looking out to sea, although some fittings were incorporated into the headmaster's house.

Masters from Rossall School, 1863. At the back are Mr McDowall, Mr Osborne, Mr Swainson (with beard, leaning against the chapel door), Mr Phillips, Mr Beechey and Mr Sleap. The first headmaster was the Revd Canon Beechey who expressed wonder at Sir Peter's plans. 'By what persuasion he was induced to invest every penny he could raise on the speculation . . . I cannot tell.'

Knott End, *c.* 1890. Across the river from Fleetwood boarding houses were built, and an attempt was made to create a popular seaside resort called St Bernard's-on-Sea. Although people enjoyed crossing on the ferry, the village appealed mostly to golfers and sailors. Mr William Swarbrick, the skilled river pilot, came from there.

The layout of the Mount in the 1870s when the town was still unfinished. Originally marked out by plough, streets radiated from here like the spokes of a wheel. On the left is Mount Terrace where some of the earliest houses were built.

The pleasure boat stage and esplanade, c. 1899. From here visitors were taken up river. In the picture are also fishing smacks, pilots' punts nearby for going ashore and on the horizon an early steam trawler. Catches of shrimps were landed and sold on the beach.

Fleetwood Commissioners in 1876 near the contractors' engine, Fleetwood, inspecting work prior to the opening of Wyre Dock. The group includes Joseph Walmsley; Andrew Synett; John May Jameson, civil engineer; Samuel Bidder, railway engineer; Thomas Drummond, builder; and Frederick Kemp.

Emily Warbrick, a wooden, three-masted, topsail schooner in Gibson's yard, 1872. Ship building and repairs were carried out on the promenade. She weighed salted 167 tons and her dimensions were 105 ft by 23 ft by 12 ft. Originally a deep-water trader travelling to Newfoundland, she became one of the Wyre Shipping Company's vessels in a fleet of thirty-seven. The *Emily Warbrick* was later converted from a barquentine to a topsail schooner. She carried china clay from Fowey, Cornwall, until being refitted in 1937 as a cruising yacht and renamed *Lost Horizon*. Returning from the West Indies in May 1938 she was burned out at sea, but her crew were taken off by a Swedish steamer.

Maude Pickup lifeboat, *c.* 1895. Her record from 1894 to 1930 was one of the most distinguished on the Fylde Coast. Propelled with oars and sails, she was so well designed for her task that the men called her 'the finest thing that ever sailed on salt water'. Thomas, Jack, William and David Leadbetter, Billy Croft and Coxswain Bob Wright are in the boat holding oars. In her career she saved 117 lives and on 16 June 1897 made history by rescuing eighteen men from three wrecks. On that occasion the crew, known as 'the cockleshell heroes', were Tom Perry, Nicholas Abram, 'Judy' Wright, Dave Leadbetter, Toby Wright, Coxswain Jack Leadbetter, Second Cox Dick Leadbetter, Jim Roskell, John Salthouse, Charlie Hughes, Matt Boardman, F. Bettess, Matt Cowell and Lawrence Bond.

A Mediterranean water pot which probably fell from one of the cargo ships that visited the port between the 1870s and the 1890s. It was dredged up from the River Wyre and presented to Fleetwood Museum. On another occasion a valuable bronze cannon of antique origin was found. Unfortunately this was sold to a Birmingham firm and not preserved for posterity in Fleetwood Museum. The numerous items found or presented locally include the coffee grinder from Drewry's shop on Dock Street, which ground fresh coffee for Queen Victoria when she came to Fleetwood in 1847.

One of a pair of blue and white china vases which were washed up in the eighteenth century when the *Traver Indiaman* was wrecked off Rossall. They were taken to Rossall Hall as it was then the right of the Lord of the Manor to claim all such flotsam and jetsam. A charter dated 28 July in the reign of Henry III granted the Abbot of Dieulacres the manor of Rossall 'with its appurtenances together with wreck of the sea'. A hoard of Roman coins found in a brick field near Rossall Hall was also taken to Sir Peter's home in 1840.

The Mount Summer House, 1838. The ten-sided summer house was occupied by Esau Carter Monk, one of the earliest of the Fleetwood Commissioners appointed under the 1843 Improvement Act. Esau, who was a humorous character, served refreshments to visitors. To make it more attractive the large sand hill was grassed, and paths, shrubs and flower beds were laid out. Traditionally the ship's mast has endured as a symbol since 1836. The hollow at the foot of the Mount was a favourite place for picnics and open-air dancing. Pharos Street, Victoria Street, London Street and Bold Street radiated from the Mount. In later years a pavilion replaced the pagoda-like summer house, which was also known as Prophet Place. On the tip of Rossall Point, in the distance, can be seen the Landmark.

The steamboat pier and station at the turn of the century. Fleetwood railway station, the ferry, the back of Queen's Terrace and the corner of Euston Park are sharply delineated. The large bowling green area was the archery ground in the early years of the town. Passengers sailed to Ireland, Isle of Man, Scotland and Barrow from the steamboat pier adjacent to the busy, yellow brick station. When opened on 15 July 1883, this was considered one of the finest railheads in the country, although it has now entirely disappeared. On the right is Pharos Lighthouse which, with the Lower Lighthouse and Wyre Light, was lit for the first time in 1840.

A group of fishermen attending classes in seamanship, Piel Island, 1897. 'Professor' Scott was one of the instructors. In the front row from left to right are: Tom Perry, Nicholas Abram, 'Judy' Wright, Tom Leadbetter. Second row: Joseph Leadbetter, Toby Wright, Dave Leadbetter (cox). Back row: Jim Roskell, John Salthouse, Charley Hughes, Matt Boardman, F. Bettess, Matt Cowell, Lawrence Bond.

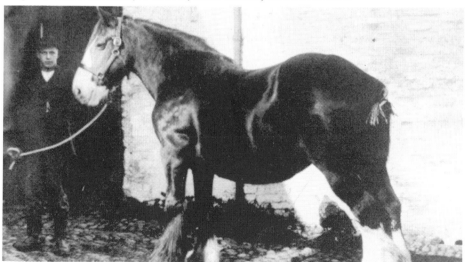

Daisy, a fine shire horse, 1911. Bred at Bourne Hall Farm, her halter is held by Cecil Cowell, son of farmer John Cowell. John also had a herd of prize Friesian cows. Bourne Hall and Flakefleet farms provided horses for processions. Strong horses were invaluable for pulling the lifeboat, the fire-engine and for work on Wyre Dock.

'Daddy' Glass, centre, with Mrs Minnie Glass, 1925. The group of Morris dancers he so diligently trained became a local legend. He was also a clog dancer and great walker, competing in the Manchester to Blackpool race in 1930 when he was 60 years old. Clifford and Eliza Glass are also in this group.

The Congregational Church in West Street, *c.* 1900. Builder Thomas Drummond started construction in July 1847 but this was delayed when the north gable and roof framing were destroyed by a gale in September. Topped by a castellated tower, the building could hold 600 people.

The Victoria Hotel, Dock Street, *c.* 1900. A glass-roofed billiards area was added at about this time. Built in 1841, like the Crown and the Fleetwood Arms, it was used for meetings of the commissioners before public buildings and halls were available. The Whitworth Institute and Estate Office were next door.

This early 1900s postcard of Bold Street leading towards the Mount gives a good idea of the tree-lined boulevards envisaged when the town was first planned. The street was named after Sir Peter's uncle, Bold Fleetwood Hesketh. London Street leading to the docks was also tree-lined.

Wyre Dock, *c.* 1890. On the left is the Fleetwood Grain Elevator of the Lancashire and Yorkshire Railway Company. Three-masted barques and a steam trawler are moored alongside. The amount of timber visible is a reminder that Fleetwood was then a busy grain and timber port.

Pioneer townspeople William, born 14 June 1835, and Jane Lambert, born March 1844. They had seven children of whom the youngest, Thomas, was born on 27 May 1882. The family moved to Fleetwood from Pilling. Before marriage Jane was a Curwen, a family involved in the timber trade.

Jack Dyer and Philip Kay, the last two skippers from the days of sail, in 1888. Both these well-respected men rode in a landau in the procession to celebrate Queen Victoria's Diamond Jubilee. Led by Philip Kay, 'Admiral of the Fleet', sixty smacks sailed out with the tide. Jack and Philip wear old-fashioned sea boots, 'Fearnought' trousers and guernseys – typical seamen's clothing of last century. Stockings and boots were heavily oiled to make them waterproof. There were a number of recipes favoured by 'old salts' for this purpose as well as for the 'barking' of the sails. Sails were laid out in the streets to dry and dyed a reddish-tan colour so that when the fleet of smacks set off to the fishing grounds it presented a most picturesque sight.

84 Mount Street in the 1960s. Although modernized, this property is an example of the terraced houses built in wide streets between 1840 and 1842. A cellar is evident and from the Ordnance Survey map of this date we learn that many cellars had a well to provide the family's water supply. In 1842 Mrs Hesketh wrote from Lytham to her husband Charles: 'Last night I heard strange things touching Fleetwood Railway . . . Vantini's hotel closed! For some time moonlight flittings numerous and every workman of every kind paid off. A family has returned to Lytham who settled in Fleetwood, literally beggared and starving.' The years of failure resulted in many cellar dwellers, as evidenced by the Census returns of that time.

Entrance to Jubilee Pier, c. 1904. By this date the Preston and Wyre Railway had passed to the London and North Western and Lancashire and Yorkshire Railway companies. The notice points out that the road is private, entry being 'on sufferance'. The hut alongside belonged to the Lancashire and Yorkshire Railway Company Police. Further left was the level-crossing for the railway which in those busy days connected with Wyre Dock station.

The Fleetwood Commissioners outside the original Custom House in 1911. They managed to purchase this building on Queen's Esplanade for use as a Town Hall because Alexander Carson who lived there had gone bankrupt. The conveyance was made on 15 October 1886. The cost of the building was £1,620; the commissioners always drove a hard bargain. In 1912 the Local Board of Twelve took over management of the town.

West Street and East Street in the 1890s. By 1911 this main thoroughfare was renamed Lord Street. The name was favoured because Southport's Lord Street had become famous. The tram route followed Lord Street and North Albert Street to the promenade, leading away from Church Street and Dock Street, once the main shopping area.

Staff of the *Fleetwood Chronicle*, *c.* 1880. Launched by William Porter on 11 November 1843 and printed on a hand press in a room above a stable, the *Chronicle* sold for 3d. It gave a clear picture of the town's growth, misfortunes and happy days, faithfully reporting meetings of the commissioners and Local Board together with shipping news.

The gravel weigh hut with cranes on the slate slip, 1908. By the iron foot-bridge is the lighter *Rossall* which scooped gravel from the River Wyre to be unloaded into waiting railway trucks. The first ferry slip was sited alongside the iron foot-bridge (demolished in 1972) on which fishermen used to whet their knives.

SECTION TWO

Harvest of the Seas

Sir Josiah Stamp and the kipper girls, 1927.

Aboard a steam trawler in the early 1930s. Clad in oilskins, the men have shot two slack hauls and eased off after bringing the catch aboard. There were astonishing catches of hake in 1905 and in 1909 *Kitty* and *Defender* brought in 440 halibut. From a fleet of six fishing smacks in the late 1830s, the industry grew into the largest fishing port in the north-west and the third most important in England. The Fleetwood Fishing Company was founded in 1841. Two families, the Wrights and the Leadbetters, controlled fish sales. Boats were built on the beach by firms like Singleton's (founded in 1842), J. Armour and Sons (1880) and J. Gibson and Sons. In the early days small-masted sailing boats ventured 15 miles into Morecambe Bay, to hurry back with a few stones of fish which they sold on the beach to residents and visitors. By 1860 there were thirty-two smacks ranging from 25 to 50 tons each, built at an average cost of £500 and by 1876 there were eighty-four sloops. Until the introduction of steam trawlers a steady ninety smacks were maintained. Fish auctions were inaugurated by Mr H. Melling.

Altering the height of the dock sill, *c.* 1930. Pictured here after completion, this required the carefully controlled use of dynamite and involved a large number of navvies, workmen and civil engineers. There were fights in dock-making days: 'Irish navvies knocked constables down like ninepins,' reported one old sailor. As cargo trade declined at the turn of the century the timber pond was turned into the fish dock. It had no lock gates but a market on three sides with concrete slades 2,000 ft long and 70 ft wide. Coaling facilities, fresh-water hydrants and salt-water pumps for washing down were available. The Fylde Ice and Cold Storage Company manufactured 34,000 tons of ice a day in huge tanks and conveyed it from factory to ship as crushed ice to be shot directly into the trawler's fish room.

Lumpers walking the plank ready for unloading *FD 269* on a snowy day in the late 1950s. At this date the port was still flourishing. Eighty deep-sea trawlers, the largest carrying crews of up to twenty men and with the ability to trawl depths of 350 fathoms, worked Bear Island, the White Sea and the Norway coast.

A huge halibut comes ashore in the 1960s. This was a time when 1,200 townspeople had jobs because of the trawlers. Cod, haddock, plaice, sole, halibut, turbot, hake and a variety of other fish were landed. Costing from £120,000 to £300,000 to build and put to sea, and from £150 to £300 per day to keep them there, the first deep-freeze Fleetwood trawlers could stay at sea for up to four months. (Courtesy *Blackpool Gazette*)

John Robert Leadbetter, who was said never to have had a day's illness in his life, was both seaman and lifeboatman. He is leaning against the post from where he fired warning signal maroons to summon the lifeboat crew. He served as coxswain and assisted in saving 186 lives. In 1891 he was one of the crew of the *Child of Hale*, from 1892 to 1894 of *Edith* and from 1895 to 1924 of *Maude Pickup*. From the same family Thomas Leadbetter of 16 Flag Street, born in North Meols, is listed among many fishermen in the 1851 Census. Peter Leadbetter was the oldest person in 1895 at a gathering 'represented in the town by five generations, he being 87 years of age'.

'Couch' Wright approaches Jubilee Quay in *FD 112 Judy* with his catch of prawns, *c.* 1941. This was another of the well-known fishing families which settled in Fleetwood last century. 'Couch' carried ashore exhausted men from the wreck of the *Commandant Bultinck*. There were also Roskells, Bonds, Rimmers, Sumners, Thomasons, Heskeths and a plethora of nicknames: Smasher Jackson, Red Neck Lombard, Rhubarb George, Danish Peter, Dutch Harry, Rising Tides, Fly Holmes, Snarler Edwards, Big Fred, Whiskers Hesketh, Bung Colley and Pepper Wright. The iron wharf designed by Robert Stephenson was in use by 26 March 1844. Costing £21,000, it included capstans, cranes and warehouses. Two bonded warehouses were provided in Dock Street.

FD 200 *Star of Freedom*, coal-burning trawler in the 1930s. Fishing companies such as Kelly's, Marr's, Ward's and Kelsall's continued landing their boats until war broke out in 1914, when most were requisitioned for mine-sweeping duties. German bombardment of the east coast sent Grimsby boats to the north-west. With its harvest from the sea totalling £1.5 million in 1910, Fleetwood was recognized as the premier hake port of the country but concern followed in the next year when stocks declined. Even *Punch* was interested and put into verse the proposed exploratory trip by the *Florence Brierley* organized by the Fleetwood Fishing Vessel Owners' Association to find rich replacement fishing grounds:

> I am informed a piscatorial mission
> Starting from Fleetwood is to undertake
> A thorough scientific inquisition
> Into the life and habits of the hake.

Fleetwood fish merchants on the fish stage, July 1925. Fish boxes of the type shown were in later years replaced by aluminium kits. This photograph caused quite a stir because of the ghostly image on the right. The men in the group said it was Mr Haig who had packed fish with them and died only twelve months before. Fishermen are notoriously superstitious and believe that the spirits of their dead mates can return, especially in times of trouble such as a storm at sea. Spiritualist and author Sir Arthur Conan Doyle was interested. The *Sunday Express* psychic notes reported: 'The publication of the Haig photograph has brought details of other cases where, with no apparent medium present, extra figures have appeared on the plate.'

Steam Trawler *Don* with a small sailing boat alongside in the 1920s, a time when trawlers were battered by 80 m.p.h. gales in the Irish Sea. It was feared that *Dean Swift* had been lost until a telegram was received from the Isle of Man to say all was well.

Edouarde Anselle 0 158, a Belgian trawler, passing the grain elevator in the very early days of the Second World War. Mr and Mrs Van Beirs were among those Belgians who fled from Ostend to Fleetwood when Hitler overran Europe. Mrs Van Beirs was the daughter of a Belgian trawler owner, Armement Ostendais.

Gutting the fish on deck, *c.* 1920. These Fleetwood fishermen have shot their trawl and after emptying the cod end are gutting the fish prior to packing them in ice on the way back to port. Fish livers were separately processed at Isaac Spencer's factory.

The New Docks Curing Company in Sidings Road, 1925. The girls are preparing the fish for curing and salting. Two thousand men and boys were employed in landing, packing, icing and provisioning the fleet and coaling. A further 1,200 were employed in allied trades: marine engineering; splitting and curing houses; fish-oil and fish-meal factories. (Courtesy *Blackpool Gazette*)

Gava, the Fleetwood trawler, sailed from Fleetwood on 27 May 1940 in command of five others trawlers: *Dhoon, Edwina, Evelyn Rose, Jacinta* and *Velia*. On 1 June at 12.24 she left Dunkirk with French troops on board, having been under enemy fire. At 1.05 p.m. crew men A. Munn, H. Gawne and J. Jones dived overboard to rescue three wounded French sailors.

A sea bird alights on *Cuirass* in 1929 amid nets, catch, otter board and other tackle, watched by skipper Mr Anderson. Seagulls in particular followed the trawlers into port, swooping down for any scraps as fish were sorted into barrels on the dockside. In 1928 *Cuirass* went to the aid of the doomed *Briarlyn,* wrecked off St Kilda, when Bill Brewster was skipper.

Staff outside Richard Irwin and Sons Ltd, Fish Merchants and Curers, Wyre Dock, c. 1922. A similar number were employed at the Fleetwood Dried Fish Company Ltd, which specialized in smoked haddock, kippers and bloaters, while the Neptune Fish Marts Ltd offered 'wet, dry, smoked and cured, pickled and fried fish'.

The Fish Stage, Wyre Dock, c. 1930. Among the trawlers being prepared for a voyage are some owned by Moody & Kelly. Icing by chute is in progress. Montagu Higginson & Company and George B. Jackson supplied bunker coal for steam trawlers along with the Wigan Coal and Iron Company. Fishing gear and provisions came from Taylor & Tomlinson and J. Preston & Sons, and clothing from Cosalt and Trawler Supply.

Fleetwood Chronicle staff last century, with a bowler-hatted reporter on the left. Tide tables, news of the arrival and departure of vessels, storms, railway information, and even lists of visitors in the 1840s and '50s were all reported. Outstanding events like aviation week and the unprecedented storm of 'Black Friday', 21 December 1894, called for special supplements.

Trawler *H.E. Bates* off the rocks at Islay, *c.* 1920, where *Margaret Wicks* and *Cormorant* went aground. The skipper of *Red Charger*, Mr J.T. Snape, sailed his ship through a reef barrier off Glas Island, Islay, in 1948 in the teeth of a gale to rescue the crew of the *Roden*. During the rescue operation Snape was on continuous duty for forty-two hours. *Fanny*, *Angle*, *Cartagena* and *Gaul* were all casualties of the 1920s' gales.

The *May Baxter* in the 1940s with Mr T.F. Chard in the foreground. Since the end of the last century overfishing of the oceans has been a matter of concern. The size of the mesh in netting is now controlled so that immature fish are not taken but allowed to grow and propagate. As early as 1899 Professor Charles Jackson referred to the necessity of farming the sea.

Twenty-three of the thirty-two children left destitute after the storm on 2 October 1895. Five Fleetwood fishing boats were wrecked, drowning eleven men, eight of whom left widows unprovided for. Some of the men lost at sea were Robert Wright, Robert Fleming, John Aughton, William Scott, Thomas Wright, John Ball and James Wright. The Relief Committee launched an appeal.

The 41-ft twin-engined Watson class lifeboat *Ann Letitia Russell* tows trawler *Northfleet FD 226* on 15 March 1967. In the 1860s Captain Swarbrick assisted becalmed smacks and the early lifeboats in his tug *Wyre* when galeforce winds made progress by oars and sail impossible. The town founder's ideal was for 'a great community with the true spirit of comradeship'.

The schoolgirl on Lifeboat Saturday, 1929, became Mrs Crosthwaite. There were so many Wrights and Leadbetters in Fleetwood all hailing from pioneering days that this photograph, taken outside the lifeboat house, was referred to as 'a right [Couch Wright] and a left [H. Leadbetter]'.

Wireless operator Lawrence Bond (front) with deck hands on board at the end of a three week fishing trip in Icelandic waters, c. 1969. They had sailed through and photographed ice floes, fortunately in relatively calm seas, to return with a good catch in the fish room.

From *FD 289 Urka* in 1972 is a view of Wyre Dock and the open channel. The crew assembled prior to setting off, and waved farewell as they passed the Watch House. White handkerchiefs were never used because to the superstitious they were reminiscent of shrouds. Late crew members anxious to have a parting drink at the Fleetwood Arms were known to dash up at the last minute and leap aboard as the trawler passed through the narrow dock entrance.

Maple Leaf leaves Fleetwood for the last time in April 1953, bound for Ceylon. The 346-ft trawler, one of Boston Deep Sea Fishing and Ice Company's fleet, was initially known as *Boston Attacker*. *Samuel Hewett*, the last of the steam trawlers, was towed out of Fleetwood to be scrapped in October 1968.

Gourock Rope Works, *c.* 1920, where Miss M. Carter was the last supervisor. The girls were kept busy net braiding and the men making ropes. Eventually plaiting and braiding by hand could not compete with steam machines so these industries died out.

The lifeboat house and promenade in 1906. This was a popular place to watch the trawlers setting off and returning. Notice the ice cream barrow in the foreground from which penny cornets were sold by the 'hoky poky' man, Monsignor Ventello.

Three Fleetwood smacks, *Beaver*, *Harriet* and *Comet*, arrived in the harbour on the morning of Thursday 7 February 1895 after passing the night in a snow storm and blizzard. Beyond Jubilee Quay in the background are signals and railway trucks.

Skippers, managers and telegraph boys photographed in October 1927 when celebrations were afoot to commemorate the fiftieth anniversary of the opening of Wyre Dock. At the North Euston Hotel a luncheon was served to ninety guests invited by Sir Josiah Stamp, the leading railway official. Both Wyre Dock and Fish Dock were open to the public daily.

Sailing smacks in port, 1914. Mr Marriott's statistical information on Wyre Dock and Fleetwood details the changes that year. 21 May: 'The fish stage on the north side of the New Fish Dock was extended, estimated cost being £21,424.' This provided thirteen additional berths for trawlers. Sailing smacks traditionally tied up at Jubilee.

The 1,718-ton stern trawler *Northella* owned by J. Marr & Son, 1967. The 245-ft trawler based at Hull was the biggest ever to land fish in Fleetwood. At that time one of the most modern in the fleet, she was equipped with every electronic, navigational and fish-finding aid. Northella had the industry's first all-metal fish hold. Note the quadpost mast which with one brisk tap of a hammer could shed a load of ice. Until recent years the nightmare of all trawlermen was that of top-weight caused by icing of mast and rigging. This could capsize the vessel which meant certain death for the crew. In February 1982 J. Marr & Son reported a 2,286 kit catch by the *Gavina* which was worth £55,518, the most successful catch for six months. The *Gavina*, which fished the western grounds, was commanded by Jeff Sumner, and the French fishing adviser Jean Pierre Claudal was also on board. Marr's manager Jim Cross was jubilant and expected that the company's Fleetwood operation would continue with this kind of success. Unfortunately in April of the same year the lumpers' refusal to land more than one trawler a day at Fleetwood forced them to arrange for landings on the east coast where *Norina* grossed £26,001, *Idena* £23,724 and *Jacinta* £48,350 in one week.

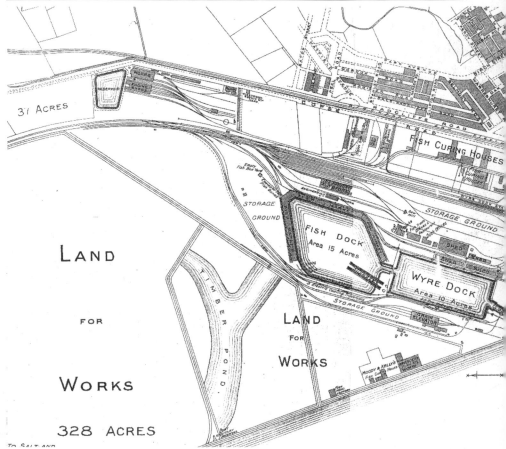

31 ACRES

FISH CURING HOUSES

STORAGE GROUND

FISH DOCK
Area 15 Acres

STORAGE GROUND

SHED

LAND

WYRE DOCK
Area 10 Acres

FOR

TIMBER POND.

LAND

STORAGE GROUND

FOR

WORKS

WORKS

MOODY & KELLYS

328 ACRES

TO SALT AND

Plan of Fleetwood Docks issued in 1922 when the new Fish Dock was completed. At the same time a map was published showing Fleetwood in relation to the fishing grounds and principal inland fish markets to which fast train services could deliver the fish. The plan shows clearly the proximity of town to docks and the fulfilment of ideas drawn up 100 years earlier by architect Decimus Burton and Sir Peter Hesketh Fleetwood. The radial plan of streets from the Mount degenerated into a typical utilitarian grid pattern, but it was the making of the Docks which brought prosperity. The unexpectedly high cost of railway construction had almost bankrupted the founder in 1844 so the original concept was shelved. Note the important part played by the railway, engine sheds and reservoir, the steam saw mills, fish curing houses, grain elevator, china clay warehouse, fish meal factory and port hospital. This plan implies a whole town involved in the fishing industry. Using the latest facilities fish were discharged direct from vessels on to slades at the dock side. Then, at special berths away from these slades, appliances placed ice, coal and stores on board trawlers for a quick turn around. Catches were rapidly sorted, laid out for auction and within hours loaded into trains, arriving at Billingsgate (for example) the same morning. On nearby slipways trawlers could be painted and repaired. The progress of the steam trawling industry at Fleetwood had been phenomenal. Firmly established as the premier fishing port on the west coast, its natural, well-sheltered harbour and excellent geographical position

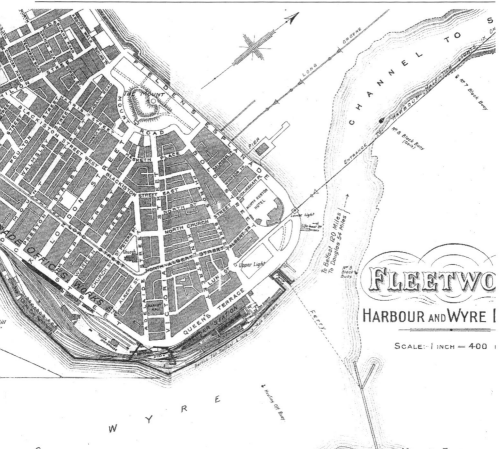

ensured success. The new Fish Dock was undoubtedly the finest of its kind in the world. To north, south and west of the port lay extensive fishing grounds tempered by the warm waters of the Gulf Stream, ideal breeding places for all kinds of fish. With close proximity to fishing grounds, cheap coal and dock dues, operating costs were low. Quick to realize these advantages, east coast merchants diverted to the 'fishing port of the west'. Some were drawn by its famous advertisement issued by the Fleetwood Fishing Vessel Owners Association. 'Fleetwood fish is the finest, freshest and firmest fish. It is free from all disease, being found full fifty fathoms deep in flowing, foaming sea by Fleetwood's famous fishermen.' On and on went the slogans, feeding from two letter Fs, ending, 'Only foolish people fail to fry, and feast on Fleetwood's famous fish.' It was a statement of the confidence and immense pride felt by the whole town. The withering away of this great industry was brought about by the loss of distant-water grounds following the cod war. By 1979 the deep-sea fleet was down to nineteen trawlers compared with one hundred only a few years previously. 'The Icelanders pushed us beyond the limit where the fish go too deep for us,' said one top skipper. Trawlers were scrapped or sent to other ports, skippers forced to invest money in small boats for inshore fishing. The end of Fleetwood as a deep-water port affected far more than the crews. For every man at sea there were over a dozen support workers.

Wyre Gleaner FD 269 stranded on the Tiger's Tail in March 1976. This was a treacherous sandbank feared by trawler skippers hurrying for port on a fast-ebbing tide. *Wyre Gleaner* was unable to move until the next flood tide. Before harbour improvements deep-water anchorage was possible in the natural basin of Canshe Hole. (Courtesy *Blackpool Gazette*)

Icelandic coastguard vessel *Arvakur* attempts to cut the warps of the Fleetwood trawler *Gavina* during the cod war which waged intermittently in the 1960s and 1970s. Collisions occurred between Icelandic boats and our trawlers in spite of Royal Air Force and naval patrol helicopters keeping watch. The loss of equipment and catch could run to thousands of pounds.

The Resort – People and Events

'Greetings from Fleetwood', a 1909 picture postcard.

A visitor to Fleetwood in the early 1900s. Gwen is known to have stayed at the Crown Hotel and called on her Irish relations in Kemp Street prior to catching one of the mail steamers, *Duke of York* or *Duke of Clarence*. Many Irish people settled in Fleetwood, escaping the 1840 famines and cholera epidemics. Others emigrated to America. Old residents recalled the funnel colours of 'the Dukes', black with white band and polished copper steam pipe. Every evening except Sunday the Royal Mail steamers left for Belfast. Between 1910 and 1912 the berths 2, 3 and 4 used for the British Mail and cargo vessels projected out into deep water. The Isle of Man services used berth 1, the most northerly, constructed in 1891–2.

Mr W. Piper, *c.* 1906. A frequent visitor to fellow photographer Mr Howorth who produced hundreds of Fleetwood views and portraits, Mr Piper, whose father established himself as 'artist in photography' in 1858 in Camborne and Hayle, thus combined business with pleasure. Both men produced views of their respective towns, using whole plate glass negatives. Photographer Mr Nickson had an order from Fleetwood Urban District Council to print 500 photo engravings of town scenes in 1899 when a determined effort was being made to popularize Fleetwood as a holiday resort.

S. PETER'S PARISH CHURCH, FLEETWOOD

A
PUBLIC MEETING
WILL BE HELD IN THE
ALBERT HALL,
On Monday, February 20th, 1888

To consider the question of providing a set of Harrington's Tubular Bells
for the Parish Church.

YOUR ATTENDANCE IS EARNESTLY REQUESTED.

The Chair will be taken by the Vicar at 8 o'clock.

W. H. ASHTON, Printer and Stationer, 14, Dock Street, FLEETWOOD.

A public meeting was held in February 1888 in the Albert Hall to consider obtaining a set of Harrington's tubular bells for St Peter's as the parish church did not have a peal. They were eventually purchased and fitted but were not a complete success and so fell into disuse.

Blackpool Fire Brigade in the 1890s when the Water Witch engine helped to put out fires in Bispham and Fleetwood. The first official but inadequate Fleetwood Fire Brigade arrived in 1868 although a set of rules and an old manual engine from Rossall Hall dated from 1848. Kemp & Company and the Railway Company 'rang their bells hastily as fire alarm bells'.

The old Lifeboat House in 1936. Demolished in 1976, it was constantly threatened by storms, one of which almost washed it away. Launching the lifeboat was a problem because of sand collecting on the slade. Note the cannons brought by Sir Peter Hesketh Fleetwood from Tulketh Hall where his aunt lived.

Mona's Queen II, c. 1900, affords a better view of the cannons, one of which fired a welcome to Queen Victoria. Mr Porter, the customs officer, was standing by. Launched in 1885, this iron paddle steamer, 328 ft in length and with a gross tonnage of 1,559, was built by the Barrow Steamboat Company. It was disposed of in 1929.

The schooner *Old Hunter* was wrecked at Fleetwood off Shell Wharf in 1906. On 20 February the *Maude Pickup* lifeboat espied her in difficulty at 'The Neckings' and took off her crew of four. On the following day schooner *Maggie Kelso* was also rescued by *Maude Pickup*.

The barque *Clara* was carrying timber when she was wrecked in December 1906. The signal gun fired from the Lifeboat House awakened the whole town. Because of the gale Coxswain Leadbetter requested the *Fylde* to tow the lifeboat to the wreck. Captain Peterson and crew, fearing capsize, had taken to a small boat and had to be rescued from a sandbank.

Empress Queen, c. 1899. Another of the Isle of Man steam packet boats sailing from Douglas, she was 380 ft long and built of iron. Launched in 1897, and wrecked at Bembridge, Isle of Wight, on 1 February 1916, her loss was due to enemy action.

Rossall Hall which became The Northern Church of England School for the sons of clergy and gentlemen in 1844. A frequent visitor when 'ye small lorde of Rossall' (one of Sir Peter Hesketh's ancestors) lived there was Squire Thomas Tyldesley who liked to come 'a sea-pye hunting' after which the company played cards into the small hours.

The beach, Fleetwood, *c.* 1904. The boy with the stick is Herbert Ramsey. In the distance is a paddle steamer, possibly the *Prince of Wales*; to the right is the Liteboat House erected 1897 and the Lower Lighthouse. Across the River Wyre at Knott End is the Bourne Arms Hotel and Sea Dyke. 'Bracing, healthy climate; unqualified facilities for boating and fishing . . .': such advertisements encouraged late Victorian crowds to take a train to the comparatively new seaside resort within easy reach of Lancashire and Yorkshire. Cheap trips on the railway were available throughout the holiday season. Activities included watching the shipping from the promenade or the Mount, regattas, dancing on the Warren and programmes of sport. Athletic sports included bicycle and foot races, egg gathering and a one-mile handicap, while football matches were 'under the auspices of Fleetwood Rangers Football Club'. Trips out to sea or up river were other attractions as were the firework displays in late September. At Hambleton there were large mussels for sale.

A group of four Edwardian ladies including Alice Lightbown photographed in Ash Martin's Studio, Adelaide Street, *c.* 1907. (Fashions were described in the *Fleetwood Express* 'Gossip for Ladies' column.) The photographer's brother, Captain Martin, was a master mariner in Fleetwood.

Promenade & Pier, Fleetwood.

The promenade and pier, 1911. Note the wrought-iron weighing machine by the seat and, far right, the end of the North Euston Hotel after the removal of its bath houses. This photograph was taken soon after the Pier Pavilion opened, when the convict ship *Success*, raised from Sydney Harbour, was on view at Jubilee Quay.

Five generations of a Fleetwood family in 1902. From left: Margaret Helen Hargreaves, Catherine Haslam, Margaret Arkwright and far right the great-great-grandmother of baby Elizabeth standing beside her. 'Granny Gregson' was from Rossall Grange Farm near the Landmark.

Ploughing with two horses at Brade's Farm early this century. One of the Brade brothers was a fireman in the Wyre Dock Fire Brigade. Horses were indispensable on farms and for the railway and docks. Fleetwood had four blacksmiths in 1866 and eight by the 1900s.

Dolly's Cottage, Knott End, in the 1920s. Close by was Sea Dyke where the pilots boarded vessels going up the River Wyre. Visitors loved to photograph the thatched dwelling and partake of 'Old Doilee's teas'. Dolly was born in 1811 to John Hodgkinson and his wife Margaret. Altogether there were nine children: five boys and four girls. William, born in 1813, lived until 1889, the great-grandfather of Mr Harry Hodgkinson of London. Dorothy, 'Doilee' or Dolly as she was known, married Richard Riley, a Fleetwood pilot and settled in this cottage, built in 1719. Their first child, Thomas, was only fifteen months old when Richard, his father, was drowned, swept overboard one stormy night. Dolly, the widow, managed by setting up a tea shop in her low-eaved cottage. Thomas, an enterprising boy, was apprenticed to a joiner and later opened his own joiner's shop, eventually owning saw mills. An amazing attraction at Dolly's Cottage was the parrot in a large cage; brought from foreign parts by a sailor, it could swear fluently.

Loading lorries and vans with supplies outside the Steamer Hotel, October 1927, the year of the flood which devastated Fleetwood. A high spring tide was driven by gales to 7 ft 9 in above the normal level. The sea poured into 1,223 houses, isolating the town. Food was conveyed to the inhabitants by boat.

An incident referred to locally as 'Klondyke', 1926. Residents were digging an area, once a coal dump near the North Euston Hotel, for whatever scraps of fuel they could salvage. A general strike took place between 3 and 13 May 1926 which meant that no deliveries of coal were made to houses and trawlers lay idle. (Courtesy *Blackpool Gazette*)

Mount Grounds and Esplanade, Fleetwood.

The Model Yacht Pond and Bridge, Fleetwood.

The Marine Gardens, Fleetwood.

The Childrens Paddling Pool, Fleetwood.

Greetings from
FLEETWOOD

Greetings from Fleetwood in 1934 pictures the Mount, the Mount grounds, the model yacht pond, the children's paddling pool and Marine Gardens. All these improvements were made for the charter year of 1933.

Tram Terminus &
Pharos Lighthouse, Fleetwood.

In August 1905 the tram terminus and Pharos Lighthouse printed on a scallop shell was a favourite card for visitors to buy. On the extreme left is the cottage hospital which had moved to purpose-built premises from Queen's Terrace in 1895.

The beach and North Euston Hotel, 1918. The large crowd gathered in front is no doubt watching an August regatta. The splendid hotel, known in early days as 'the wonder of the place', was a crescent, designed by architect Decimus Burton to give maximum sea views. On 10 January 1850 the hotel was designated Royal North Euston, the occasion being a public dinner when Fleetwood was constituted an independent port. Sir Peter Hesketh Fleetwood gave a speech and a special 'wedding cake of the Port of Fleetwood with the ocean at large' was displayed. The flax and sail-cloth trade of nearby Kirkham had attracted the interest of the Emperor of Russia. The government used this hotel as a School of Musketry of which Colonel Halliday was Commandant in the 1860s. Unfortunately later demolition of the bath houses which were situated to the right spoiled the shape. Once patronized by an emperor, dukes, earls and the nobility of the land, as the fortunes of the town declined it was closed for a time.

Louie Rigby FD 127 competing in the Coronation Regatta at Fleetwood on 24 June 1911. Organized by the Blackpool and Fleetwood Yacht Club, the first event at 9 a.m. prompt was a handicap race for deep-sea fishing smacks. Competing with *Louie Rigby* owned by W. Preston were *Surprise FD 122* owned by W. Leadbetter, *Onward FD 17* also owned by W. Leadbetter and *Harriet FD 111* owned by Henry Leadbetter. It was an exciting race with a first prize of £15 won by *Louie Rigby*. Crowds gathered by the Watch House at Steep Breast to see W. Stoba, starter for the races in the Regatta, line up the 'famous four'. The Victoria Pier manager claimed that 'the best view of the Regatta will be from Victoria Pier'. Other events included climbing the greasy pole for which the prize was a leg of mutton and 7s 6d, walking the greasy pole, swimming races, sailing races and a Scratch race for Fleetwood pilots' sailing punts. Fleetwood Town Band performed throughout the day in Euston Park and prizes for professional events were distributed at the North Euston Hotel at 8 p.m.

In the 1890s the Fylde Cricket Club had fixtures in Fleetwood. Cricket was played from the 1840s onwards, with games held on the Warren. Other sports including wrestling matches and wheelbarrow races were also played here. Stephen Burridge jun., a customs officer, was treasurer of the Fleetwood Cricket Club and Mr Lofthouse, a chemist, was a keen supporter.

The Sea Wall Swifts, c. 1950, played at the Highbury Speedway Ground where racing began on 13 April 1948. Behind the netting of the goal posts can be seen the crash barriers. David Cookson, centre forward, has the football and Tom Ball and Eric Cranston are also in the group. The Skate Nob Warriors of 1908 featured Crewdson, Manning, Bond and Bellwood.

Rossall Grange Farm in 1927 after the great flood on the night of 29 October. A sheep has been rescued but many others as well as horses and pigs were lost. Eventually six people died. Schoolmaster Charles Gaie collapsed from a heart attack and caravan dwellers Lily Bailey, Mary Chard and children James, Richard and Ellen were drowned. They were the family of Charles Chard, mate of a steam trawler.

Marsh Mill, *c.* 1918, built in 1794 by Bold Fleetwood Hesketh. This tower windmill with an external platform at third storey level had a Bees Flyer fantail and 30 ft common sails. Restored to working order, it is now the central attraction of a multi-million pound shopping complex opened by the Duke of Westminster. The 200th anniversary of Marsh Mill is to be celebrated in 1994.

The sloop HMS *Fleetwood*, May 1937. As the ship approached, large crowds waved hats and handkerchiefs and greetings were signalled from the Mount. Each day the ship was inspected by an average of 8,000 people and officers and men were given the freedom of the town, thereby cementing a bond of friendship. Commander A.C. Chapman and his officers received a civic welcome at the Town Hall and every day of the week was full: Monday, civic welcome; Tuesday, dinner given by the Fleetwood Fishing Vessel Owners Association who presented a handsome silver cup; Wednesday, Corporation dinner; Thursday, 'At Home' on board ship; Friday, the crew were guests in the Marine Hall. On the Wednesday, because it was Queen Mary's birthday a royal salute of twenty-one guns was fired. The Town Clerk, Mr J. Bell, the Mayor, Alderman W.E. Simpson and the Deputy Mayor, Alderman Charles Saer and a line-up of Fleetwood Grammar School scholars stood alongside HMS *Fleetwood* moored at the quay.

Fleetwood Market in the early 1950s. This famous market, created under rights granted by Henry III in 1235, opened on 7 November 1840 in the presence of Sir Peter Hesketh and Lady Fleetwood. Large numbers of cattle were brought to be sold at the cattle market, first on the *Thomas Dugdale* then on the Irish boats until the cessation of the service in 1928. The Fleetwood Estate Company bought the market in 1875 when it consisted of a paved area surrounded by a high sandstone wall. Two heavy wooden gates opened on to Victoria and Adelaide Streets. As the market prospered the Improvement Commissioners wanted to buy it for the town and finally succeeded. By 1933 a Longridge-stone market hall, shown in this crowded scene, had been built containing ninety-four stalls with hiring charges varying from 1s 6d to 5s 6d. Murals by Mrs Jean Mann were painted in the 1960s. Today the entire market area is covered.

The Mount Pavilion, *c.* 1910. The Chinese pagoda known as Prophet Place or Temple View was replaced by this pavilion. In later years the firm of James Robertson presented a clock and anemometer in memory of the men who died in the First World War. The Mount, originally Tup Hill, was a traditional meeting place even before Fleetwood was built. On 20 May 1861 an angry crowd, incensed that an ancient right of way was threatened by enclosure, tore down part of the surrounding cobbled wall. Sir Peter Hesketh Fleetwood agreed to retain one quarter and give the residents three quarters, the Commissioners promising to maintain the wall. In the 1870s it passed entirely to the town and Queen Victoria's Diamond Jubilee was celebrated here with a processional crowd carrying silk banners. The annual ceremony known as the Blessing of the Waters is conducted from the pavilion balcony.

The ferry, Fleetwood, *c.* 1930, with a steam trawler and the ferry boat *Wyresdale* loaded to the gunwales drawing away from the ferry slip. Acquired under the Fleetwood Improvement Act of 1893, the ferry issued 500,590 tickets in the most popular years, 1932–3. Originally ferry boats ran from the stone jetty opposite the Whitworth Institute.

Bourne May arriving at the ferry slip, Knott End, *c.* 1912. In the background can be seen Fleetwood railway station, the lighthouses, North Euston Hotel and the Lifeboat House. John Gibson & Sons completed the *Bourne May* on 1 June 1900 at a cost of £1,846 and in December she was launched by James Armour & Sons.

Pile driving, *c.* 1907, during the construction of Fleetwood Pier. Richard Edmondson, a Fleetwood Commissioner who had fought since 1892 to acquire a pier eventually left the town in despair. The second attempt was opposed by the railway company and the pier was not built until 1910. The Prospectus and Plan of 1906 shows Tom Lumb as architect and Gradwell's of Barrow as the builders.

The Free Pier, Fleetwood, 1937. 'The first thing the holidaymaker looks for is the pier,' said Richard Edmondson. Artistic entrances, turnstiles, kiosks, cloakrooms, a 200-ft timber jetty, ornamental bandstand and a handsome pavilion drew the crowds.

Lancashire comedian George Formby in the Marine Hall, Fleetwood, in 1942, after judging the final of the first Miss Great Britain beauty contest. His wife Beryl holds a bouquet. The Formbys lived in Poulton-le-Fylde where George was a member of the Home Guard during the Second World War. (Courtesy *Blackpool Gazette*)

Solly's Concert Party performed on the beach in the 1900s. The paddle steamer *Mona's Queen* is off to the Isle of Man. Ventello's Oyster Bar is on the beach nearby. To sit and watch the concert cost 2*d* but most people stood by the promenade railings while a member of the cast 'went round with the hat'.

Pleasure craft in the River Wyre, *c.* 1900. The Fleetwood Steam Pleasure Boat Company agreed in 1901 with the Railway Company over the landing stage. 'Charming indeed is Fleetwood in the height of summer, with its cool sands. . . . Two hours' steaming takes the tourist across Morecambe Bay. As a bathing place it possesses very superior attractions.' (*Round the Coast* 1902)

The ferry and beach in 1929 show a busy summer with many customers for the pleasure boats going up river or to view Wyre Light. The ferry boat left with a full complement on most trips to Knott End, where wagonettes waited and homemade ice cream was obtainable at the Bourne Arms.

In the 1900s houseboats permanently moored on the shore at Knott End were popular in the holiday season. Many of these were made from fishing boats which were no longer seaworthy and some became permanent homes. Mr W. McNciry of Knott End ran wagonette trips which left from the ferry slip and skirted the shore as the tide receded.

Fleetwood swimming pool in the 1930s also affords a view of the Pier Café and full length of the pier before its destruction by fire. The open-air pool was a chilly experience except during the heat wave of August 1939 and has now been replaced with magnificent indoor facilities.

Commandant Bultinck, a Belgian trawler, wrecked at Rossall Point on 2 October 1929. Rossall schoolboys along with their teachers helped to rescue the crew but one young man was drowned. He was buried in Fleetwood cemetery and for years a Fleetwood lady tended his grave.

RMSS *Viking* viewed from across the River Wyre, June 1925. Berthed behind the railway station, there was a special walkway for passengers to embark on this 'crack ship of the Line with triple screw turbines' built in 1905 by Armstrong Whitworth & Company.

Captain John Quilliam, RN (1771–1829) aged 58, was the ancestor of a Knott End man, Mr C.F. Doughty. John Quilliam ran away to sea and was apprenticed under Captain Quayle of Castletown on the *Ellen Vannin*, a Manx brig which plied between Mediterranean ports. Quilliam and five other Manxmen were press-ganged to serve on a British warship. He was an outstanding seaman who quickly rose to midshipman, seeing action in the battles of Camperdown, Copenhagen and the Nile. At the Battle of Trafalgar he was commended for outstanding seamanship while under enemy fire. In 1967 his ornamental dress sword was discovered behind panelling and his compass, sea chest and telescope have been preserved. His great-great-grandson C.F. Doughty became a gunner in the Merchant Navy.

Situated on the corner of Preston Street and Lord Street, Lofthouse & Company Ltd gave a face-lift to the premises established by one of the town's early chemists in 1865. In the 1840s George Laurie and Henry Albright were the first chemists. Mannex's 1866 directory records James Doughty, chemist. Laurie was agent for a series of marine signal lights patented by Robson & Higham but he was declared bankrupt as the fortunes of the town declined sharply. With the departure of Sir Peter Hesketh Fleetwood, burdened with debts, all building stopped and there were many business casualties and much hardship in Fleetwood.

A bazaar held in Fleetwood in 1913 in aid of the Fielden Sailors' Rest. It was in this year that it became the Royal National Mission for Deep Sea Fishermen. With financial help from Mrs Fielden of Todmorden the old building was replaced.

Harvest Festival at the Fielden Sailors' Rest situated on the corner of London Street and Dock Street. Mr W.H. Dickenson, port missionary, stands in the centre. In 1894 Fleetwood had a branch of the British and Foreign Sailors' Society. The Bethel in Kemp Street cared for shipwrecked sailors.

Stanley Baldwin with his wife Lucy, accompanied by Lord Stanley, son of the Earl of Derby, visited Fleetwood in September 1929 to canvass support for the National Government. They dined at the Mount Hotel. Lord Stanley was MP for the Fylde.

Captain Lord Stanley lays a foundation stone, *c.* 1929, close to premises which became the Church Army Youth Club built on the site of the old Testimonial Schools, erected in 1847. The stone crest of the Fleetwood Hesketh family was preserved from the schools' building and placed into the Mission premises by Colonel Roger Fleetwood Hesketh, a descendant of Sir Peter.

The flood in October 1927 in the Poulton Street area. This lorry took supplies to householders as the waters subsided. As some houses were flooded to ceiling height initial delivery was by rowing boat past bedroom windows.

Fleetwood Borough Council on 2 June 1953 when the corporation arranged a programme of events to celebrate the Coronation of Queen Elizabeth II. Front row from left: C.D. Skeoch, mace bearer; Alderman C. Saer; Councillor G. Penkeyman; Alan Smith, town clerk; Councillor J.W. Robinson, mayor; Councillor E.A. Lawrence, deputy mayor; Councillor E.M. Hope; Alderman W.E. Simpson.

The Rialto Dance Band in the 1930s was led by Harry Longworth, with Wally Birch as saxophonist, Tom Birch as trumpeter and Joe Gatehouse on banjo. They played at the Marine Hall as did Dan Ellwood with his big band. Bob White's band for whom Mrs Edie Sumner was pianist were known as the Serenaders. They entertained American troops at Weeton Camp. (Courtesy *Blackpool Gazette*)

Fleetwood British Legion Dance Band performed at the British Legion Headquarters which opened in 1928. The British Legion Club was struck by lightning in September 1930.

Two houses built for gas workers in 1840, demolished in the 1960s. Demolition of houses in Mount Street and Cop Lane was carried out under the Slum Clearance Act. Of the 1,000 sq. ft of land reclaimed, two units were sold for industrial purposes. Fleetwood was supplied with gas from 1840 but there was much dissatisfaction. When Queen Victoria arrived in 1847 the Lower Light failed as the royal yacht approached the quayside, supply being unequal to demand. Mr T.A. Drummond, a builder, chaired a meeting in 1857 demanding 'good gas at a fair price' and said that 'it was nothing better than sewer gas'. Mr Beesley the gas manager was fined £20. The *Fleetwood Chronicle* editor in 1882 scathingly advised: 'Content yourselves with paraffin oil and the primitive dip.' (Courtesy *Blackpool Gazette*)

Fleetwood Police Station in Victoria Street next to the market has now been demolished. Large new premises which include a magistrates' court have been built on the promenade. The first police station was in Flag Street. James Fowler became the police sergeant when Sergeant Crean was promoted to inspector at Kirkham.

John Clarkson, headmaster (left), and Charles Saer, assistant master, with Standard Seven boys outside the Testimonial School early this century. The schools were erected in honour of Sir Peter Hesketh Fleetwood and for many years on their anniversary the bust of the founder was decked with a laurel wreath.

A crowd gathered in the shadow of the Lower Lighthouse to celebrate the Coronation of Edward VII in 1901. Flower-trimmed Edwardian hats were damaged by the heavy rain as Mr Howorth took the photograph.

Decorations along the promenade in 1933 when Prince George presented the Charter of Incorporation to the mayor, Councillor George M. Robertson. For a time the corporation allowed £2,000 for the cost of illuminations to prolong the season.

Crowds stranded outside Fleetwood railway station on 19 August 1911. This was due to a general strike when trains and other public transport ceased to run. Mothers and children were put up overnight at the Empire Theatre and Hippodrome, which was built in 1898 and later became the Art Cinema.

Fleetwood Coronation procession on 22 June 1910. The banner is passing the Empire Theatre on Lord Street surrounded by a group of schoolchildren. Note the tram standards which then ran down the middle of the sett-paved road.

THE GUV'NOR
AT FLEETWOOD

'The Guv'nor at Fleetwood'. This postcard, sent 'Friday morning 3 August 1928', was one of many in the 'Seaside Comic' series. Fleetwood post office was kept busy with telegrams from fish merchants which were delivered by dozens of telegraph boys until Wyre Dock got its own post office.

Three well-known scenes in the Fleetwood of the 1930s: 1. View from the bandstand in the Marine Gardens where deck chairs were hired; 2. Memorial Park, laid out in the grounds of Warrenhurst, once the home of John May Jameson, Civil Engineer to Sir Peter Hesketh Fleetwood; 3. Landing stage, Marine Lake. The Marine Gardens and lake were among improvements to bring Fleetwood up to borough status. Joe Corrigan had a joy wheel and marionettes for the children in the Marine Gardens.

Deserted platforms at Fleetwood railway station in April 1966. At precisely 8.56 p.m. on Saturday 16 April the last train pulled out, ending a railway era of 126 years. Inspector R. Ryding and the railway staff's farewell was expressed in a series of cracking detonations as diesel M 50958 glided along the track. The train was driven by Leslie Skinn, a 72-year-old retired driver. On board were thirty-two passengers including the deputy mayor, Councillor E.H. Funk. Bob Etherington, who brought the first diesel train into Fleetwood in 1959 and who had worked on the railway since 1910, was also on board the last train out of Fleetwood.

The royal visit to Fleetwood of George VI and Queen Elizabeth (now the Queen
Mother) in May 1938. After their coronation in 1936 the king and queen travelled
throughout the United Kingdom to meet their subjects. The scene is outside the Marine
Hall and the umbrella held by Lord Derby protecting Queen Elizabeth was most
necessary. Hundreds of children assembled to see the royal couple got very wet, but
their enthusiasm was not damped. Mayor Charles Saer and Mrs Saer acccompanied the
king and queen who chatted with ex-servicemen outside the Marine Hall, opened by
Lady Stanley in November 1935. (Courtesy *Blackpool Gazette*)

The boating lake, *c.* 1936, was used to stage a water carnival and in 1949 the Entertainments Committee arranged for a 'mermaid' to come ashore at the ferry slip and travel in triumphal procession along the promenade to Robinson Crusoe Island in the middle of the lake. Rowing boats and small sailing yachts could be hired; nowadays it is popular for wind surfing. Each year it was drained, cleaned and refilled. In the 1960s chemicals had to be used to kill off the invasive growth of spartina grass which rapidly developed on beaches in the Fylde. The Sea Cadets had a boat permanently moored for training. The model yacht pond which adjoins became internationally famous, with yachtsmen from as far away as America, Canada and Japan coming to compete annually.

Mona's Isle, travelling from the Isle of Man and approaching Fleetwood in 1980 on an ebbing tide, became stranded in front of the North Euston Hotel. The masters of the Manx boats experienced difficulties as the channel began to silt up in spite of regular dredging by the *Bleasdale*. She was the fourth vessel of that name owned by the Isle of Man Steam Packet Company Ltd. Originally called *Onward*, she was purchased from the South East and Chatham Railway, refurbished and put into service in 1920. *Mona's Isle I* was launched in 1830 and disposed of in 1851. *Mona's Isle II*, afterwards *Ellan Vannin*, was launched in 1860 and lost in 1909.

The monument in Euston Park, seen here in 1982, was erected in memory of James Abram and George Greenall, fishermen who lost their lives trying to save others in the storm of November 1890. People gathered in the vicinity of Euston Park to wave goodbye to the trawlers and fishing smacks which in return signalled 'Cock a doodle doo' goodbyes as they sailed past the promenade. It was considered appropriate that the granite boulder in front of the obelisk should be inscribed in memory of seamen. Chosen by Lionel Marr of J. Marr & Sons Ltd, the granite boulder embodying the tough and rugged qualities of seamen was engraved by Alfie Hopton, a local stonemason, 'in memory of all those who lost their lives at sea'. The plaque was unveiled by Admiral Sir Desmond Cassidi on 19 May 1982 at the start of Maritime Week. (Courtesy *Blackpool Gazette*)

MARINE GARDENS, FLEETWOOD.

The Marine Gardens in front of the Mount were a blaze of flowers in the 1960s when Mr Ernest Chantler was head of the Parks Department. When tides were high the sea once came up to the base of the Mount but tide changes allowed land to be reclaimed.

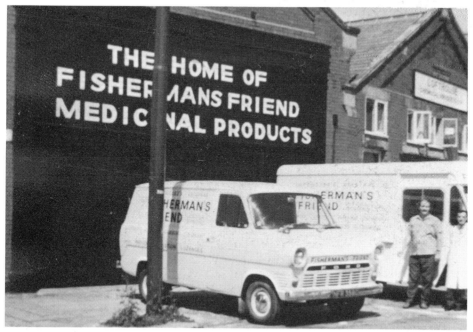

Lofthouse of Fleetwood Ltd has grown into a £60 million company since chemist Mr Lofthouse made Fisherman's Friend cough lozenges in 1865. These premises next to the North Euston Hotel were occupied from 1968 to 1972. By the van is director Tony Lofthouse, first right. The company has since moved to huge purpose-built premises in Maritime Street.

A Wellington bomber crashed into the sea in front of the Mount in 1945 after passing over the town and skimming the Marine Hall. All the crew were killed. On a receding tide children reached the wreckage with its grisly contents before the police and other authorities arrived. Memento hunting went on for days. During the Second World War the whole area of the beach was spiked with broken railway lines and sleepers, hammered in to prevent enemy landings. All that Fleetwood suffered from German bombardment were five high-explosive bombs, the first incident being on 11 December 1940. Two bombs were dropped on railway premises. One fell in the timber pond (a smaller pond having been made after the original became the Fish Dock), the other in a railway siding. Fortunately no one was hurt in either incident. (Courtesy *Blackpool Gazette*)

Blakiston Street during the great flood, October 1927. In the background is Blakiston Street Infants' School. Mention was made of the flood in the school log-books. Captain James Calvert of Willow Street reported: 'A tremendous wave burst open the door and carried me into the roadway. I was swept away for a distance of 150 yards into Poulton Road. I managed to grasp the sill of a window bay. Those inside dragged me in.' Mr Dunderdale, a caravan dweller near Copse Road, narrowly missed drowning by climbing on to the roof of his caravan and escaping on an improvised raft. Boy Scouts and Fleetwood St John's Ambulance men conveyed foodstuffs from the Congregational School and the police station, the two distribution points. In Radcliffe Road and Blakiston Street houses were flooded to a depth of 7 ft in a few minutes. Extra police who came to the town were billeted in the Co-operative Hall. The fire engine was used to pump water out of houses on the fringe of the flood.

Fleetwood pier going up in flames, 20 August 1952. This was the biggest fire in the history of the town and flames could be seen for 20 miles. Thousands of residents and visitors watched the spectacle from 10.30 p.m. until midnight. The fire was thought to have started behind the cinema screen. Councillor E.F. Michie of Windsor Terrace along with hoteliers and holidaymakers smashed in the doors, formed a human chain and dragged out whatever they could rescue. Damage costing £40,000 reduced the pier to a tangled network of steel girders and charred timbers. Eight fire engines attended. Next day fortune hunters scrambled beneath the pier, salvaging coins fused together by the inferno. Previously the biggest fire had been the one on 28 October 1926 which destroyed the fish oil works of Isaac Spencer Ltd. In 1952 the pier was open all year round and claimed to be the only carpeted pier in the world. With its cinema, ballroom and jetty enclosure, Victoria Pier had been the mecca of Fleetwood holidaymakers. (Courtesy *Blackpool Gazette*)

Mayor Making, an annual ceremony since 1933 when Fleetwood became a borough, was staged for the last time in 1973 as local government reorganization had resulted in the formation of the Borough of Wyre comprising Fleetwood, Poulton, Thornton-Cleveleys, Garstang and district. Some of the splendid regalia including the mace and the mayor's chain of office, both presented by the Derby family, passed to the new borough. Mr Charles Skeoch was mace bearer from the time when the town was first incorporated. Fleetwood had worked hard to achieve non-county borough status and townspeople did not welcome the change. The great moment when Prince George handed over the Charter of Incorporation had been watched by 12,000 people in the Marine Gardens; the celebrations lasted for days. Lord Derby was present and at the luncheon that followed a telegram was received from the king wishing the town every success. (Courtesy *Blackpool Gazette*)

Town criers from all over the country assembled in Fleetwood in the 1960s for a contest outside St Peter's Parish Church, organized by Fleetwood Chamber of Trade. The lady in this photograph is grandmother Jean Wells from Dorset. The judging panel consisted of the deputy mayor and mayoress and Councillor David Baker. The winner on this occasion was Noel Phillips of Devon. Annual events brought more visitors. There were beauty contests, Lorry Driver of the Year competitions, the Blessing of the Catch, Hospital Saturday processions, displays by the Sea Cadets, a Real Ale Festival, bowling championships and music and drama festivals. Early Fleetwood featured military bands from the School of Musketry, the morris dancers trained by 'Daddy' Glass and Harry Stonestreet's 'Doodah' Band. (Courtesy *Blackpool Gazette*)

SECTION FOUR

Shops, Business, Wyre Dock

Bird's-eye view of Wyre Dock, 1910.

Pharos Lighthouse, 1908. Designed by Decimus Burton and lit for the first time in 1840 along with the Lower Lighthouse and Wyre Light in the Channel, Pharos was sandblasted in the twentieth century to reveal the original sandstone. This did not please the Isle of Man Steam Packet Company. Captain Ronan complained: 'Now it is no longer white it is not as clearly visible.'

The Lower Lighthouse seen through the portico of the North Euston Hotel, 1940. Placed in line with Pharos, the two lights, one above the other, guided mariners into the River Wyre. Sailing directions were charted by Henry Mangles Denham in 1840 when he used the yacht *Fleetwood* to make soundings. 'The Wyre is a good, safe river,' he reported, but unfortunately the removal of the knotts, or groups of stone from Knott End led to the impairment of the river's natural scouring action.

Schooners of the Wyre Shipping Company assisted into port by tugs in 1903. The company, owned by Edmund Porter and Richard Warbrick was the registered owner of thirty-seven schooners ranging in size from the 86-ton *Nanny Wignall* to the 200-ton *Lizzie Porter*. Others were *Red Rose*, *Dairy Maid*, *English Girl* and *Richard Warbrick*.

An original copy of the *Fleetwood Chronicle* for Saturday 1 February 1845. Fleetwood steamships for Glasgow, Belfast and Londonderry and 'the cheapest and most expeditious route to Glasgow via Fleetwood' were regular prominent advertisements. Exports from and imports to Wyre Dock are listed within.

This young man (name unknown) worked in the 1900s at the shipbuilding firm of James Armour, famous beyond Fleetwood. William Stoba, their ship's architect, patented his curved forefoot which made for better handling and greater speed. He fitted this to vessels *Alpha* and *Kindly Light*. The latter, renamed *Theodora,* was until recently competing in the Tall Ships Race. James Armour and his wife Ann came to Fleetwood from Londonderry in 1847. Born in 1817 and a blacksmith by trade, he died on 24 January 1875. His son James married Elizabeth Gill. They had eleven children, one of whom, James, married Catherine Whiteside who bore him fourteen children. This James recorded in his diary: 'Started work for my father on 28 December 1886, aged 13. John Armour, my uncle, died on 3 January 1869. He was one of seventeen survivors of SS *London* which foundered in the Bay of Biscay in 1866.'

The Lifeboat Station with an RNLI official in 1981. Situated on the promenade, this office and shop together with the lifeboat pen in which the *Lady of Lancashire* is now kept permanently afloat, was constructed after the old lifeboat house was demolished and some of its timbers burned on the beach. *Lady of Lancashire 44 - 015* was launched by the Duke of Kent in July 1976. His Royal Highness took a sail in Morecambe Bay in the new lifeboat accompanied by Dick Willoughby, Customs Officer, and other officials.

Grace Wright, aged 20 at Christmas 1916, worked in the office of R. Newton & Sons Ltd, established in 1870. Their head office was on Dock Street but they also had premises on Wyre Dock. Ship repairers, boat builders, shipwrights, joiners and blacksmiths, they were on the Admiralty List. Filed away in Grace's office was the following indenture: 'Made 1 January 1858 between Robert Newton of Fleetwood, aged 16 years and James Newton, father . . . and John Gibson . . . ship builder etc.' John Gibson paid Robert Newton 3s a week for his first year of apprenticeship and 10s a week at the age of 22.

Marz RE 261 entering dock, *c.* 1950, a medium or middle trawler for work off Iceland, the Faroes and the White Sea. Voyages lasted from thirteen to sixteen days and the hold would carry about 40 tons of fish.

Leader and *Falcon 1 F* and *2 F*, pilot cutters, are in the background of this 1920s scene as a small cargo boat sails past Knott End towards Wyre Dock. Coasters *Lithium*, *Barium* and *Thorium* came regularly from Wales with supplies for Imperial Chemical Industries at Burn Naze.

Visit of the Newfoundland Prime Minister, Sir Edward Maris, to Wyre Dock in the early 1920s. The Premier is the figure in the centre. A trade agreement was drawn up followed by a tour and inspection of Wyre Dock.

The old timber pond in the 1870s before it became the Fish Dock. In the background is the grain elevator of the Lancashire and Yorkshire Railway Company. The wrought-iron bridge can be seen more clearly in the bird's-eye view of Wyre Dock on page 118.

The Moody & Kelly vessel *New Crown*, moored alongside *Delta* in the 1870s when Wyre Dock was a forest of masts. The first vessel to sail to the West Indies from Fleetwood was the *Sarah Trotman* in 1845, but as cargo trade increased ships went all over the world, to San Francisco, Canada, the Baltic and Shanghai.

A typical Wyre Dock scene in 1910. The figure near the coal trucks of the Wigan Coal and Iron Company is possibly Tom Blacklidge, Dock Manager. The method of landing fish had altered little: block and tackle pulleys hauled up baskets from the fish room and lumpers then walked the gangplank with their loads.

Mr A. Turner holding a 5-ft cod weighing 5 stone which was caught off Iceland in September 1960 by the Fleetwood trawler *Red Knight*. Men who had worked all their lives at Wyre Dock said they had never seen a bigger cod. Sister ship *Red Hackle* represented the deep-sea fishing fleet at the Coronation Review at Spithead on 15 June 1953.

Trawlerman's family (name unknown), *c*. 1921. The dangerous calling of fishermen led to much hardship. After the storm of 2 October 1895 a meeting was held and a Relief Committee set up with Councillor Davies JP as Chairman, Councillor R.C. Ward as Hon. Treasurer and Mr R.F. Addie as Hon. Secretary. One lady was bought a clothes mangle so that she could support herself and family by taking in washing. Christmas Day 1925 witnessed a lifeboat rescue in the midst of a howling gale. Morecambe Bay was suddenly lit up with distress flares. Three miles north of Wyre Light the 6,000-ton liner *Tchad* had dragged anchor. Three Fleetwood men were among those on board. The crew had been detailed to take *Tchad* to Heysham for breaking up. With flares exhausted, the captain ordered mattresses to be set alight, and guided by the flames the lifeboatmen battled through the storm to reach the exhausted men.

Fisherman's Friend (extra strong lozenges) vintage van in the 1960s with the Mount Pavilion and cobbled wall made from Fleetwood seashore pebbles in the background. This van carries sales teams across Europe, Scandinavia and Japan. The company, Lofthouse of Fleetwood, exports to seventy-five countries and has won the Queen's Award for Industry in 1983, 1989 and 1993. Their new factory on the Industrial Estate occupies 200,000 sq ft. One of Fleetwood's oldest trawlers, the *Cevic FD 7* (1 2 4 5 7 8), still appears on the packaging of Fisherman's Friend lozenges. Built in Aberdeen in 1908, this trawler was owned by the Cevic Steam Fishing Company Ltd. and sold in 1953.

Other long-established businesses included: Brown & Jackson (1908), Great Grimsby Coal, Salt and Tanning Company (1873), James Robertson & Sons (1883), John Jackson & Sons (1875), W.H. Ludlam (1875), J. Preston & Sons (1847), H.E. Howorth (1895) and William Hodgkinson (1888). In the most prosperous days of the town there was a Fleetwood Granite Company, a cheese and a button factory and F.E. Carter had a mineral water works. The School of Musketry opened in 1861 with 100 acres of land earmarked for practice, a hutment, barracks and a convalescent hospital. The sixty officers and staff of instructors lived at the North Euston Hotel where the poet Wilfred Owen had a short stay just before he was killed. The First World War curriculum included courses for volunteers and adjutants.

City of Selby and *Imelda FD 13* side by side in December 1917 on the first slipway, constructed in 1893. Vessels were brought periodically for repair, scraping and painting. The 337-ton *Wyre Majestic* which collided with an iceberg in 1964; *River Doon* which made her last trip to the fishing grounds on 10 March 1950 and *Strathalva* which ran aground in the same year were all overhauled on the slipway.

Preesall old pier, across the river from Wyre Dock, 1936. Beneath the Wyre ran a pipe carrying brine from the Preesall salt works to ICI at Burn Naze. From this pier the fine quality white rock salt was exported to countries as far away as India. Salt mining caused subsidence in the 1930s and so was discontinued. (Courtesy *Lancashire Evening Post*)

Wyre Dock in a bird's-eye view of 1912, one of a series commissioned when improvements were in progress. Laden coal wagons, 8 miles of railway track, the gravel weigh huts, cranes, the lighter *Rossall*, moored trawlers and additional slipways make an interesting comparison with the plan on pages 58–9. By 1945 Fleetwood was described as a boom town. 'Money flowed from the Fish Dock. Charitable causes had their share and George Formby [see page 82] remained a frequent visitor to help good causes.' This appeared in the *Fleetwood Chronicle* which celebrated its centenary that year. Circuses were a diversion. Bostock's and Wombwell's used the North Euston ground; Bailey's pitched on land behind Noblett's Farm near the cattle pens and Sanger's on Poole's Field where the British Legion Club now stands. However, by 1950 the mayor, Councillor C.F. Lofthouse had written to the Prime Minister for help towards the fishing industry, which resulted in the setting up of the White Fish Authority.

Lord Street, 1929, the main street of a busy town. Bus no. 14 is on route 11 to Blackpool. J.W. Fish's long-established business of cutlers and tool dealers is on the left near the Congregational Church. On the right on the corner of London Street is Bradley's, boys' and men's outfitters, who then had branches in most Lancashire towns.

The Royal Oak, Lord Street, October 1927 when 2,000 tons of logs were washed down from Keay's sawmills on Wyre Dock. Hodgkinson's mineral water business, established in 1888, can be seen on the right and Ye Olde Bacca Shoppe is on the left towards the Testimonial Schools.

FD 15 in Wyre Dock in 1973. By this time grain and scrap metal were being handled as well as fruit and vegetables from Bilbao, Spain. The Dutch fleet of thirty-three, beam-trawling for sole in the Irish Sea, had finally pulled out in 1971. *Gavina* made her maiden voyage to Iceland in that year. Ships arrived from Cyprus, Egypt, Greece and the Canary Islands.

Wyresdale ferry boat, *c.* 1930, was the largest of the steam-driven vessels and cost £6,460. Built at Fleetwood in 1924 by Messrs James Robertson & Sons Ltd, she could carry 250 passengers and a crew of three. She operated with *Pilling*, a small vessel acquired for the low-water service on spring tides.

The volunteer camp, Fleetwood, *c.* 1911, showing the tent set aside as a post office. At frequent intervals during the summer, detachments of the Royal Garrison Artillery and Royal Field Artillery across the river at Knott End practised, using wrecks on Pilling Sands as targets.

An open-air Mission in 1907 with lady helpers alongside the tents. 'Camp Fleetwood' reads the caption and the van with the flag aloft advises: 'Give up sin'. These vans trundled between Fylde towns and villages, the missionaries camping where they felt the need for conversion was greatest. This site may be the cattle fields area also used by the circus.

Albert Square in 1930 is busy with traffic, trams and shopping crowds. On the left is T. Riley's ironmonger's shop, now razed. Thomas Riley also owned the North Lancs Steam Saw Mills. Behind the tram (no. 8) is Hollingsworth's Café and beyond Riley's is the long-established bakery of Parkinsons, who were also Italian warehousemen.

Bold Street in 1908 where Thomas Woods, the printer who published Porter's *History of the Fylde,* lived. He objected to the pier being built at the end of Bold Street so it was moved lower down. In this street there was a boys' academy, one of six in Fleetwood in the nineteenth century.

Members of Fleetwood Civic Society gathered in 1977 with the mayor, Councillor Greenwood, and the mayoress, Mrs Greenwood, for a ceremonial receiving of a key from Fleetwood, Pennsylvania, USA. Second from the left is Councillor Charles Kaberry next to Richard Keighly. On the right is Roger Cross, chairman of the society accepting the key. The two ladies next to him are Margaret Daniels and at the front 'Bill' Curtis. Fleetwood Town, Pennsylvania, celebrated its centenary in 1973 and Mrs Bill Curtis went to the USA to hand over mementoes from Fleetwood. Plans are currently afoot to twin the towns, thus cementing the friendship. The key is now on display at the Mount Craft Centre in the Mount Pavilion. Fleetwood Civic Society has been instrumental in saving important artefacts for the town such as the Cosalt stained-glass window celebrating Queen Elizabeth II's Silver Jubilee and the Lancashire and Yorkshire Railway's carved stone from the base of the grain elevator. The refurbishment of the Mount Pavilion itself which had been vandalized and the gilding of the cast-iron Cherub Fountain which dates from 1890 and is situated in Euston Park are also due to their efforts.

Mr Clegg outside his fish and chip shop with Fleetwood children at around the turn of the century. His 'Supper Rooms' were situated next to Bennett's, the butchers at the corner of Albert Square near St Peter's Church. In the 1960s Clegg's premises had become the Camera Centre run by Mr and Mrs Curtis.

Melias Ltd, grocers with their staff of seven outside, c. 1930. William M. Fairclough had these premises on East Street in 1866 when the town had nine grocers and tea dealers. Ann Bond, also a tea dealer, had a confectioner's shop on Dock Street. This is indicative of a rising population and the amount of shipping which had to be provisioned.

In the shadow of *Lavinda FD 159*, a vessel belonging to J. Marr & Sons Ltd, is a group of German visitors to Wyre Dock, 1968. On the right is Brian Hornby, Fleetwood's port guide. The names of Marr's Fleetwood ships at this time ended with the letter a: *Josena, Junella, Lavinda, Luneda, Navena, Velia*. It was likewise from their base in Hull that *Northella, Southella, Starella, Thornella* and *Westella* occasionally sailed to Fleetwood; thus a strong bond existed between the two great fishing ports. The first stern freezer trawler to sail from Fleetwood was *Criscilla*, owned by Marr's.

An accident at the Ice Factory extension during the dock extension scheme in 1928, when the new triple slipway was installed and the Belfast boats were transferred to Heysham, a move which stunned the town of Fleetwood. One of the worst incidents on the dock was the timber fire which broke out where the firm of Gradidge stored Stockholm-tarred logs and sleepers. A pall of smoke hung over the town for two days. There was a fire at J. Marr & Sons on 14 May 1919.

Buffalo moored at the new quay from where the Isle of Man boats also sailed, 1974. The old quay, attacked by a minute sea creature, became unsafe and the Isle of Man Steam Packet Company would not continue service until it was reconstructed. *Buffalo* and *Bison* inaugurated the Pandoro roll-on roll-off container service continued by *Viking Trader*.

Fleetwood stern trawler *Boston Blenheim* braving an Arctic storm in the 1960s. She was acting as guard-ship for the *Robert Hewett* in the troubled days of the cod war. The most notable development in trawler design was the use of stern as opposed to side fishing. The catch could also be deep-frozen on board.

The last passenger train left Wyre Dock station in 1970, since when the line has handled traffic for ICI. The group of Fleetwood Grammar School boys includes John Rothwell, Peter Cook and Peter Brook. Mr Langhorne, left, wearing spectacles, runs a book and sports equipment shop on Poulton Road. (Courtesy *Blackpool Gazette*)

'Britannia' class steam locomotive *Oliver Cromwell* no. 70013 called at Wyre Dock station on a special 1970s railway enthusiasts' run. *Ayrshire Yeomanry* arrived just before *Oliver Cromwell*, pulling a twelve-coach excursion train chartered by the Merseyside Railway Correspondents' Society. Two other famous locomotives to have run on the old Preston and Wyre line are *Mallard* and *Flying Scotsman*.

Acknowledgements

The late Tom Blacklidge • *Blackpool Gazette* • Lawrence Bond
British Transport Docks Board • British Trawlers Federation • David Buckley
Lyn Cain • T.F. Chard • David Clayton • Tony Coppin • John Dales
the late Cecil F. Doughty • Ian Fairclough • Fleetwood Civic Society
Fleetwood Fishing Vessel Owners Association
Fleetwood Fish Merchants' Association • Eddie Funk • Catherine Haslam
Peter Horsley • Louis Klemantaski • *Lancashire Evening Post*
Lancashire Library • *Lancashire Life* • Lofthouse of Fleetwood Ltd
Terry Lyons • Dorothy McClellan • Eric Mills • Peter Owen
Joan Pendlebury • Rossall Archives • Ron Severs • Ralph Smedley
RS Studio • William Ward • Tony Winfield • Skipper 'Couch' Wright
Skipper 'Devon' Wright.